Praise for *Borrowings of the Shan Van Vocht*

Catherine Moore's prose poems restore voices to figures long silenced by the bog. The Drumkeeragh Woman curses her husband's betrayal. The Haraldskær Woman dreams of a final taste of berries. The "perfectly ordinary" Auning Woman remembers aspirations of girlhood, before pit and pinned body. Some may enter by choice—"I followed the wraith winds through the labyrinth's coils," testifies the Meenybraddan Woman, "All things smeared over with night green." But most do not, and the poet has found a potent vehicle to explore entrapment and sacrifice. Consuming, preserving, the land always has the final word: "I soak the glorious cloud-water, stomach the earth flesh, ferment it to tannin, press it to peat. This is my vigil to swallow and salve." This is a moving, disturbing collection.

—Sandra Beasley, author of *Count the Waves*

It's commonly said that we are doomed to repeat history. But what if that history is buried in muck and mire? In Catherine Moore's brilliant *Borrowings of the Shan Van Vocht*, "cadavers [are] the braille of death" and time "may dissolve a coin, yet clasp an ancient book of psalms." Reimagining historical bog bodies is a feat of extraordinary imagination, and Moore's narrators here—be they ghosts or corpses, even they can't decide—are "breathless, ceaseless, eyeless, […] shadowless, useless," yes, but they also know that "There will be an accounting." Moore's chapbook is a lovely, lyrical must, and the voices therein are precise and true, beautiful and tender—these are worlds inside worlds, endangered and kissed with confessions otherwise entombed forever.

—Gary McDowell, author of *Mysteries in a World That Thinks There Are None*

Catherine Moore's collection *Borrowings of the Shan Van Vocht* breathes beautiful life into the grotesque remnants of these "bog women." By reimagining the women as they once were, Moore resurrects their power, or in many cases, gives them power to take for the first time. Their decayed bodies and resurfaced faces become emblems of both rebirth and a "second burial." Perhaps most notable is the intertwined theme of women violated and rejected by a society full of violent, demanding men, as well as of "the good men, fools and minstrels, [who] stood by." She writes of a society built with "sons that grew to love" and "daughters that grew to fear," which (when compared to today's times) might caution of history repeating itself. Her collection strives to assure the bog women that through us, the reader, their "essence is not lost in the moor's pickled sapling." Do not think that Moore's poems incite pity. The raw, visual, and wild imagined voices fight loudly against the bog, against the men, against their disappeared stories. Moore writes that "some are not right for the place they are born," which may reveal the book's true purpose—to transport these lost women into a new world. A world more fitting, more deserving, more connected to their stories. At least, we can only hope.

—Bryanna Licciardi, author of *Skin Splitting*

Borrowings of the Shan Van Vocht

By Catherine Moore

Borrowings of the Shan Van Vocht
Copyright©2020 Catherine Moore
All Rights Reserved
Published by Unsolicited Press
Printed in the United States of America.
First Edition.

All rights reserved. Printed in the United States of America. No part of this book may be used or reproduced in any manner whatsoever without written permission except in the case of brief quotations embodied in critical articles or reviews.

Attention schools and businesses: for discounted copies on large orders, please contact the publisher directly.

For information contact:
Unsolicited Press
Portland, Oregon
www.unsolicitedpress.com
orders@unsolicitedpress.com
619-354-8005

Cover Designer: Peter F. Lorën
Editor: Chandler S. White

ISBN: 978-1-950730-27-8

For Mary and Nora, my Irish Grandmothers

Poems

Bog Body Murmurs	10
Auning Woman	11
Borremose Women	12
Camnish Woman	13
Cladh Hallan Womyn	14
Derrycashel Woman	15
Derrymaquirk Woman	16
Dröbnitz Girl	17
The Wind Concurs	18
Drumkeeragh Woman	19
Elling Woman	20
Frærmose Woman	21
Girl of the Bareler Moor	22
Girl of the Uchter Moor	23
Haraldskaer Woman	24
Huldremose Woman	25
Koelbjerg Woman	26
The Sun Questions	27
Lindow Woman	28
Luttra Woman	29
Meenybraddan Woman	30
Stidsholt Woman	31
Windeby Girl	32
Yde Girl	33

Zweeloo Woman	34
Shan Van Vocht Answers	35

Borrowings of the Shan Van Vocht

By Catherine Moore

Bog Body Murmurs

In the encyclopedia of ends we are named for the bog, melting and churning, that exhumes us. Our stories within the tarn are tale-less. We are the many lesses—breathless, ceaseless, eyeless, fruitless, garbless, merciless, noiseless, ribless, shadowless, useless. Our only study is the wet. Only loss is the sun's grope overhead. We become gourds of gurgled mud with murmurs that only nudge the insides of moors. When we rise, will they say corpse or say body? It matters not. Our spade-cut skin never heals, cadavers being the braille of death.

Auning Woman

I ended as *blót*, planted as a wetland offering—blossom and blood. *There is little sacrifice in her death*, I heard my father whisper to the men. *Perfectly ordinary looking*, I told them with a pout in my unremarkable mouth. *See, she's neither comely nor ugly*, my mother pleaded. Instead, there was Ingrid, or gaze the angelic Astrid. Yet, it was I bound and taken away, my common shape of a head held high, my duck face, a nubby size of nose. As a girl, I wished for *skønhed*—the turn of eyes and heart's smile. I had lived plain and spinstered. Once doomed, I wanted wart and dagger, revolting, dangerous as a witch. To be an omen so brooding, no brutality could end me. They dressed me for the underworld in elk skin cape, mink shawl. I first thought I'd hang in dedication to Odin. On a windy tree, nine long nights, in old custom. But it was a pit for the Mother Goddess where they pinned my body, arms, and legs. They pitched the blessed peat on top of me staked down in worship. At the end I suffocated in grace, muscles clenched in convulse, spewing myself to myself, and I believed I was desired. And sacrifice.

Borremose Women

He spent his hours pretending to cut peat. Digging at the same spot. A memorial to her in pitch, mud, and wind. It wasn't the right spot, though. I watched him looking out at the horizon each dusk, his boots interned where he thought she lay, and their dead child in a jar. I let him select his own gravesite. If she thought she could birth the *nyfødte* on the bog where they met, I let her. Squat, sweat, and pant that August night. When she cried for birth, she was close to death. This was planned. The soil cooperated. When she disappeared, he sentineled like a Danish Mastiff. I knew the first blizzard would not stop him. I knew by spring thaw, the soil would suck him. I rehearsed the crack of his skull. I dreamt the growl in his strangled throat. It all happened in a blind of black and snow—flurry, fury, and fear. *Ja*, I did. I didn't expect the bog to take me too.

Camnish Woman

I formed a lump in the turf the size of my shadow. The salivating earth waited to eat bones. Before I expired, I murmured blessings as my last rites. May the oxen used to haul my body be ridden to death by demons. May a fortnight of darkness in day hours fall, and neither sheep nor shepherds return to their farms. May disease seep this village. May the parents all pass and the children wander free. May a sorceress, found to be earth-cloved and kohl-eyed, slouch into their dreams.

Cladh Hallan Womyn

I am more than I seem. *Sluagh*, as the clansmen say. A jaw that does not fit and never ceases impressing its displeasure. The thick femur that rubs this pelvis to an ache. A skull that can't quit echoing in the chaos. I am curled fetal as a body, but in unnatural articulations. Someday all that oddly rests here will be unearthed in quiet reveal. That the villagers attempted to attach these bones together. That for each piece of comely tissue there came a quick dip back into bog bodies. That we were merged so often we could not preserve our skins, only these bonny bones rattling against each other. That we are sisters of different mums—none worthy of remaining intact. A meld of perfect womyn beauty.

Derrycashel Woman

The forbidding loam embalmed slowly. We are meant for decomposition. Yet in my cold flattened skin, I persisted.

Derrymaquirk Woman

Three stones marked the way home: first stone followed the lakeshore, then a turn towards the moon at the second, the last stone always chalked white. Crude lumens on the limitless peat. That last night the bog was unlit under a new moon. The stars were unusually dismal and allowed the night to shroud the ground. The baby fussed in the pitch dark. When I no longer inhaled the smell of lake water I knew I was deeper in, where the world turned turfy sour. There was nothing to do but wade forward in the soft soil. Within the weak hue, the second stone never appeared, and what appeared as dark opening, went nowhere. It felt a walk through the womb of earth, my own pulsed with its energy. Even the wee *bairn* quieted down. I pulled my shawl down to sense with my forehead, not just my feet; the chill and damp would help me find the way. I would halt, listen, and begin all over again. Feeling my way along the edge of the bog rows, I heard in its previously lifeless depths, enormous piping frogs. Then a haunt of curlews' cries. They warned, again and again, not to slip. And I heard thunder. Thunder inside a quivering ground. In a quick swell the bog moved backward a few perches. Soft peaty substances boiled up through the chinks, heaving in all directions. I rolled and was wedged in layers of mud, moss, and water. I wrapped all I could reach around the baby. Wondered who would find us in this slough of despond the next morrow?

Dröbnitz Girl

Spring death came despite the rain, the mire, the manic bursting. It marked my taint in the dirt. Met full with my aloneness, I began a certain solace—only the chore and sadness in breathing.

The Wind Concurs

I have known the bogs as holy places, felt the many dead, their names never recorded on vellum. The disappeared make no sound, only whispered in the weeds and grass. Leaf flesh, soil flesh, singing over the bones, it forms a strange keening across this barren space. All trembles at the elongated muscle of my devotion. Vast, yielding, and gray: this is the best place to bow in lingered grief.

Drumkeeragh Woman

My dear husband stole my *dauðadag*, my death day, my dream soul's journey beyond. A Viking such as I is floated at sea or sent over in pyre. Not mislaid in a bog of the infidels: slathered into their western hills like gobs of rancid brown butter. Fit for traitors and other miscreants. What mark of man silences his wife in rot here? What make of people pillage a corpse? Reave the jewelry and rend a dead woman's gown. Prosper by a plait of the bog queen's hair. From peasant to peer, a mire of thievery surrounds me. My soul will never awake, left cold boiling on this island of sump and seedbed.

Elling Woman

It wasn't the first time he had roped me. The thong at the nape of my neck, he wore it as a leather belt around his waist. An easy yoke for his chattel. When it wasn't handy, he used my plaited braid—slide the knot of it loose, coiled it at my windpipe, and whispered, *what a lovely sacrifice you'll be.*

Frærmose Woman

Were I to count them, they would outnumber the grains of sand. This psalm I repeated from inside my heavy mud tomb. Inside the sands of dark Danish badlands—always muck and minuscule beneath my feet as I heaved across it in life. That dark sand was dainty, delicate, a size I will never achieve.

Girl of the Bareler Moor

I used to say bones don't lie. Your chisel may ungrave me but a carbon-date is nothing of me. I have no voice in lab reports nor will my dimpling skin goose-bump beneath a cool dial of temperature control.

Girl of the Uchter Moor

One couldn't be too careful, if you were born bent. I acted as able labor even if I stood stunted and twist. It may have been true, the *mahr* spirit he saw in me, my southpaw, my trembling limbs, my hunched form, mine witch. I stayed out of his way mostly, off the moors. I tried to heal mother as I did the broken song birds. After her loss, it fell to me—to tend needs, to harvest the mire, to amass his bilberries. I was the one to feel *spaten's* twang on skull. He saw the devil in each part of me and exorcised them with purpose. My essence is not lost in the moor's peat pickled sapling unearthed, a miscellany of hacked flesh—a foot, a finger, a gourd for a rib cage.

Haraldskaer Woman

I dreamt I was laid out, supine, and regal posed. The townsfolk came to see me through a glass-gilded coffin. They treated me as though I was queen. The dream was a veiled ambition until the vernal sacrifice and its potential honor. I knew I would be lanced at the joints, wooden poles to pin the body down. They promised me hemlock first. A gown and royal cape. Hurdles of branches in wreath. A privileged place in the goddess's earthy bed. Laurel and infamy. If I commanded the final meal, I'd choose luscious berries. Then I'd finally sleep near the fire. I did not think of the seasons that would digest me. Not of the tar face, caul-pit teeth, or swaddled fern-hair, if I rose from the dark. I thought only of the dream.

Huldremose Woman

In turf-cutter's pulp, I may find my purpose. The rest of the earth moved just as my husband said. Burgeoning and lush. Even the salmon spawned each season. He slit their bellies and had me finger the roe. Pray for my long winter seed of a womb. I understood his belief, what bears no fruit is hewn down and cast into pits. I asked him to wait for last harvest. Pleaded it would end without pain. A worthless tomb to become bulb. Time rebirths the body as fire fuel. My second coming, lifted in leathered bruise, as the black maw's forceps baby.

Koelbjerg Woman

This land, dreary stiff of muck, would never hold me. There is no grasp in exfoliated ocean silt. No real footing for our bark huts along lake *Tissø*. We wandered in hungers for flint, bone, and horn. Speared for our fish. In my mind's eye, I lived near the birch-pine and lapwings of my youth. Iridescent greens. Purples in slow wing beat. Where the water knew its place. I stayed as he wanted to stay. In tidal flats where the elk and *auroch* were easily seen. On black river tracts where our bodies never stayed still.

The Sun Questions

Those who lived by air have fallen away—stood on a moor's edge and dropped hands into the bog palm. Turned cold-blue with the grasp, black with the vespers. Sons that grew to love the tilling. Daughters that grew to fear the reaping. They bury in the soil and are boiled into fable. And these fallen, do I detect their subtle respiration in the grasses?

Lindow Woman

I caught a murderer because his wife refused to rise. She stayed in hearth *coomb*, unharmed, vegetal mind. I crawled where the *kesh* water cheeps and lisps. Expelled his confession long due from this ruminant tarn, before my second burial.

Luttra Woman

They had my skin, these snails, mottled, etched in brown scars. As did the bloodworms slick with this oil-dark world inching for seed. And the raspberry plant roots were whiskered like an old chin. We almost looked the same underground—clay made, soft spread. My face would always be twenty, though, if it had survived.

Meenybraddan Woman

The last time I entered the bog, figures lurched in the tree line. A woman stood blindly in the old Hawthorne. Magpies in genuflect. I nearly waved goodbye. A meandrous star lit the bare gray bog. Beckoned. It seemed like falling into a labyrinth— this perambulation, these prayers. To shed the skin of sin, along a path across turf and tarn. Twisted. Narrow. I followed the *wraith* winds through the labyrinth's coils. All things smeared over with night green. I saw the airy *naiads* gracefully melt into the waters with never a splash after. The waning moon near rise. Complete silence. It was time to leave Eden and its demon will. In subtle movement, I trailed soft-bellied down over the edge of the earth-lipped fissure, and rested throat upon the gloom bottom. The water dripped and lapped in a whisper. I slithered underground. Last sights: sphagnum moss, turf root, the bower's lid.

Stidsholt Woman

He wouldn't want me to return. That is why I roamed. Why I burrowed in every available hole. I moved about in the wan hours when Olaf's sight lines were shortened. His men were in drinks. Some are not right for the place they are born. Some are not rightly placed where they're brought. My blood and brood fought our way to the table served; I was no lady. This I was reminded of each honeymoon evening, in spats, with an ugly look about him. Swollen to the size of an ox. My battle-burst tongue spoke too passionately. My skull throat resisted his grip. A cunner and vixen, I was called. With my sharp ears, I overheard "whore," "raving mad," and they said I would howl myself to death. Olaf knew my will was strong, strong enough to draw the hunger back to one's body, as a *draugar* risen from the grave in wisps of smoke or foxfire plume pushed through solid stone. Still, a soul cannot survive without a body. On the thirtieth day, Olaf removed my ring and veil, and rushed me. My headless body fell to its knees, sank into the ground where he had been standing. In the end, I was not immune to his weapons. The good men, fools and minstrels, stood by, turned their eyes at the sword. Olaf ordered them to bury my head in the bog, burn the body, and dump those ashes in the sea. No resting place, no possible self-exhumation. He wouldn't want me to return, carrying my hideous head, mouth agaped, hair tarned reddish as fox brush, eyes blackened to onyx, covering the short distance between mine moor and his howe.

Windeby Girl

My head stubbled as plucked duck skin, or shaved adulteress. Grist in an ancient mill that hides all the silage of shameful acts. Truth will rise in this forbidden bog, its red heather killing the shell-paved streamlets and quiet pools fringed with rushes where we met. Rise from the place beneath rocks and branches used to hold my body down. They will note my thumb obscenely placed between index and middle fingers. My pornographic posture. I will become numbered bones, cataloged muscle webbings, and my missing gender satchel found. There will be an accounting.

Yde Girl

Duivel! Devil, they said and I'd lurch at them so terrifying that they ran away. Deformity and grit, my awful gifts. Unpathetic, I waited for no charitable feelings. No affection. Nothing tender. Barely a warm body wanting—the schoolmaster for my carnal self. Beauty was not required for men's attentions, my sixteen years as the hideous twisted girl had taught me. Until the day the master greeted me strangely. His eyes wooden. He removed his woolen belt. The shadows behind him moved furtively, a dark form in their hand shaped like a knife. My strangled cries cut brisk by a blade. My tormented reign seemed buried. But I'd return and see them run again, my *hel-blár* face, the blue maroon hue of death, with my corpse-pale hair the tannins dyed a fiery red.

Zweeloo Woman

I was never well. Held my gaunt-self hidden and alone in the forest for thirty years. In fatherless fear, motherless madness. Until a winter's ruin forced me from my lair. A foray for the bog's berries, it damned me. Damned under rune stones, giant crush in cowardly prayer beads. Damned to the henna red hair, the damp soil smell, part algae, part bowel. Lost corpse the tarn stripped down and sucked dry. Embraced only by roots that strangled their cursed host.

Shan Van Vocht Answers

I am wise on what to devour whole, like bones, and what to leave alone—the coatings and skin on carrion and cadavers. I may dissolve a coin, yet clasp an ancient book of psalms. I am preserving, not consuming. Sacrosanct vault. I harbor. I soak the glorious cloud-water, stomach the earth flesh, ferment it to tannin, press it to peat. This is my vigil to swallow and salve. Rope, wheel, vessel, dragonfly, human hair: I practice immersion. Provide frith-stool. I'm not responsible for the strange fruit people leave behind—trove, tools, their own.

AUTHOR NOTES—

Bog, one of the few Gaelic words that made it into English, means "soft." It is a name for wet spongy ground of decomposing vegetation that covers 1/6 of Ireland. Also referred to as fen, moor, slough.

A **Bog Body** is a human cadaver that has been naturally mummified by the pressure and chemical makeup in a peat bog.

Shan Van Vocht is a phonetic transliteration of the Gaelic phrase (*tSeanbhean bhocht*) "for the land goddess." Its meaning translates as Poor Old Woman. In modern druid terms, it is similar to Mother Nature.

Bog Poems by Seamus Heaney is a collection I admire and from which I acknowledge similarities in these borrowed phrases—study was the wet, island of sump and seed bed, water cheeps and lisps, grist to an ancient mill, reddish as fox brush, bruised forceps baby, strange fruit.

To the best of my knowledge, the following notes relate to the bog bodies that I represent fictionally in voice within this collection. Not all bog bodies have reasonably known information.

Auning Woman
1–100 A.D. Found in Midtjylland, Denmark, 1886.

She was found with sticks on top of her body; it's possible that she had been pinned down in the bog to keep the remains from surfacing.

Reconstructionsts of her body deemed her 'a perfectly ordinary looking woman.'

Borremose Women
770 B.C. Found in Himmerland, Denmark, 1947-48.

Part of a collective of three bog bodies, dated to the Nordic Bronze Age, found in the Borremose peat bog: a man and two women. Evidence indicates foul play, and one woman had the bones of an infant and a ceramic jar lying nearby.

Camnish Woman
Unknown. Found in Northern Ireland, 1834.

This bog body no longer remains.

Cladh Hallan Womyn
Unknown. Found in South Uist Island, Scotland, 2001.

DNA from the skeleton's jawbone, skull, arm, and leg show that the body was assembled from various unrelated people. The Frankensteined body was originally preserved in a bog, then manipulated and reburied in a fetal position 300 to 600 years after death.

Derrycashel Woman
1431–1291 B.C. Found in County Roscommon, Ireland, 2005.

The nearly skeletonized and complete remains of a young woman were unearthed.

Derrymaquirk Woman
750–200 B.C. Found in County Roscommon, Ireland, 1959.

The skeletonized woman was found lying on her back with bone fragments from an infant near her body.

Dröbnitz Girl
650 B.C. Found in Warmian-Masurian Voivodeship, Poland, 1939.

Examination of stomach contents and pollen analysis indicates that she had died in the months of spring.

Drumkeeragh Woman
Unknown. Found in County Down, Ireland, 1780.

Body fragments and personal affects were given to a local peer, Lady Moira, who was interested in the Nordic body. To this day, only a braided lock of hair and some cloth fragments remain.

Elling Woman
350–100 B.C. Found west of Silkeborg, Denmark, 1938.

The face of the woman was poorly preserved, and there were no traces of organs inside of the body. Her braided hair remained, as did the leather cloak tied around her legs. She is believed to have been hanged.

Frærmose Woman
Undetermined. Found in Denmark, 1842.

The woman's foot was unearthed four feet under the surface of the bog. A well-preserved shoe was found with the human remains.

Girl of the Bareler Moor
260–395 A.D. Found in Lower Saxony, 1784.

Due to the over-sampling of the remains, only the skin of her chest has survived today.

Girl of the Uchter Moor
764–515 B.C. Found near Uchte, Germany, 2000.

Moora was around seventeen when she was deposited in the bog. Examination shows that she had been malnourished, had a curved spine, and had two skull fractures.

Haraldskaer Woman
490 B.C. Found on the Haraldskaer estate, Jutland, Denmark, 1835.

Her body is on permanent display in an ornate glass-covered sarcophagus because early identity theories centered on the Queen Gunnhild of Norway. Recent evidence indicates the victim died from a violent murder or ritualistic sacrifice, a theory consistent with the body being put into a bog as opposed to burial in dry earth.

Huldremose Woman
160 B.C. –340 A.D. Found in Ramten-Jutland, Denmark, 1879.

Lacerations on her feet happened near the time of death. A rope was also found around the neck of the body, which suggests that she was hanged or strangled.

Koelbjerg Woman
8000 B.C. Found near the Nerverkær-Moor, Denmark, 1941.

She is the oldest known bog body and also the oldest set of human bones. Studies show that the woman fed mainly on land plants and marine animals, such as fish or shellfish. The distribution of her bones indicates the woman possibly drowned in the lake, and the corpse's soft parts decayed while adrift in open water.

Lindow Woman
250 A.D. Found near Wilmslow, England, 1983.

Her skull fragment was originally thought to be the deceased wife of Peter Reyn-Bardt, who confessed to murder after the discovery. But after the skull was dated, it was proven to be much older than Mrs. Reyn-Bardt. He was convicted for his wife's murder anyway.

Luttra Woman
3105–2935 B.C. Found in Västra Götalands län, Sweden, 1943.

Because there were many raspberry seeds found around the stomach area, the body was dubbed *Hallonflickan* (meaning "Raspberry Girl").

Meenybraddan Woman
1500–1600 A.D. Found in County Donegal, Ireland, 1978.

Given that she was interred in a peat bog in what was likely an unconsecrated grave, she may have been a murder victim or a suicide.

Stidsholt Woman
Unknown. Found in Jutland, Denmark, 1859.

All that remains of her is the severed head. She was decapitated by a blow to the third and fourth vertebrae. Her head is on display in the Copenhagen Museum.

Windeby Girl
1–200 A.D. Found near Windeby, Germany, 1952.

A victim of an unnatural death, blindfolded and half her head shaved. Yards away, the naked body of a middle-aged man, strangled with a hazel branch and secured in place with wooden stakes, as if the two had been killed as punishment for adultery. Further examination of the pelvis suggests that this body was a young male.

Yde Girl
100 B.C. –50 A.D. Found in Drenthe, The Netherlands, 1897.

She was sixteen when, evidence suggests, she was executed or murdered. Her bog body was reputedly uncannily well-preserved when discovered (especially her hair). Scans have shown that she suffered from a spine condition known as scoliosis.

Zweeloo Woman
500 B.C. Found in Drenthe, The Netherlands, 1951.

The body consists of the bones, internal organs, and skin. She had lived with dyschondrosteosis and other signs of sickness.

About the Author

Catherine Moore is the author of three chapbooks and the collection ULLA! ULLA! (Main Street Rag). Her work appears in *Tahoma Literary Review, Roanoke Review, Southampton Review, Appalachian Heritage, Mid-American Review* and in various anthologies. She's been awarded Walker Percy and Hambidge fellowships; her honors also include the *Southeast Review*'s Gearhart Poetry Prize, a Nashville MetroArts grant, inclusion in the juried BEST SMALL FICTIONS, as well as Pushcart and Best of the Net nominations. Catherine holds a Master of Fine Arts in Creative Writing and she teaches at a community college.

She's tweetable @CatPoetic

Acknowledgements

Escape into Life: "Bog Body Murmurs," "Dröbnitz Girl," "Huldremose Woman," "Luttra Woman," "Windeby Girl," and "The Wind Concurs."

Menacing Hedge Journal: "Auning Woman," "Borremose Women," "Girl of the Uchter Moor," "Haraldskaer Woman," "Lindow Woman," and "Meenybraddan Woman."

The Piltdown Review: "Derrymaquirk Woman," "Drumkeeragh Woman," "Cladh Hallan Womyn," "Frærmose Woman," and "Yde Girl."

Riggwelter: "Stidsholt Woman."

Roanoke Review: "The Sun Questions" and "The Bog Answers."

Slipstream: "Girl of the Bareler Moor," "Luttra Woman," "Zweeloo Woman," "Derrycashel Woman."

Stirring: A Literary Collection: "Camnish Woman," "Elling Woman," and "Koelbjerg Woman."

www.ingramcontent.com/pod-product-compliance
Lightning Source LLC
Chambersburg PA
CBHW030135100526
44591CB00009B/674